Who Pooped?

in the Park

written by **Gary D. Robson** · illustrations by **Elijah Brady Clark**

FARCOUNTRY
PRESS

To my daughter, Heather.

ISBN 10: 1-56037-279-6
ISBN 13: 978-1-56037-279-0

For more information about our books, write Farcountry Press, P.O. Box 5630,
Helena, MT 59604; call (800) 821-3874; or visit www.farcountrypress.com.

Created, produced, and designed in the United States.
Manufactured by
Bolvo Yuanzhou Midas Printing Ltd.
Bolvo Yuanzhou Town Xianan Administration District
Guangdong, PRC
in April 2013
Printed in China.

17 16 15 14 13   6 7 8 9 10

"Dad? I have to go to the bathroom." Michael squirmed in the back seat.

"We'll be at our campground in just half an hour," said Dad.
"We're in Glacier National Park now."

"He's just nervous," said Michael's sister. "He thinks a bear's gonna eat him."
She growled at Michael and made her fingers look like claws.

"Stop it, Emily," said Mom. "Nobody is getting eaten by anything."

Michael was very excited about the trip, but Emily was right. He was
nervous. He had just read a book about grizzly bears. He knew how
big they could get. He also knew that a hungry grizzly bear would eat
just about anything—maybe even a boy.

"I *am* kind of scared of bears," admitted Michael.

"Don't worry," Dad told him. "We'll show you how to count a bear's toes and never get close enough to be scared."

"Here's our campsite. Let's set up the tent. Then we can go for a walk and I'll show you what I mean," Dad said. Michael was awfully worried about grizzly bear toes, but tried not to show it.

"Let's hurry!" said Emily. "I want to see some animals!"

Once the tent was up, the whole family went for a hike. Emily started to complain before they even left the campground. "I haven't seen any animals yet. Maybe there aren't any here!"

"There are definitely animals here," said Dad. "We're going to learn about them from their scat and tracks."

"Scat?" said Michael. "What's scat?"

"Scat is the word hikers and trackers use for animal poop," Mom said. "Look over here."

STRAIGHT POOP

Beavers usually poop in the water, so you won't find beaver scat very often.

"Footprints!" said Michael.

"And something else, too," added Mom. "Beaver scat."

"It looks like little pieces of wood," said Emily.

"Beavers gnaw on wood all the time," said Dad. "Their scat has lots of wood chips in it."

"They use the trees to build their dams and the lodges they live in," added Mom, "and they eat the bark."

"The scat told you what they eat," said Dad. "Now look at the tracks. Their back feet are webbed, which makes them good swimmers."

"And you can see how big the tail is where it dragged along here," said Mom.

"The tail helps them swim, too."

"See, Michael," said Dad. "We don't have to get up close to an animal to learn about it. Instead of a close encounter of the *scary* kind, we'll have a close encounter of the *poopy* kind."

Everybody laughed, and Mom made a gross-out face.

"Dad! Mom! Look over here! I found bunny scat!" yelled Michael. "It's just like what we have in Fluffy's cage."

"We came all the way to Glacier National Park for *that?*" grumbled Emily. "Michael's bunny makes plenty of poop at home."

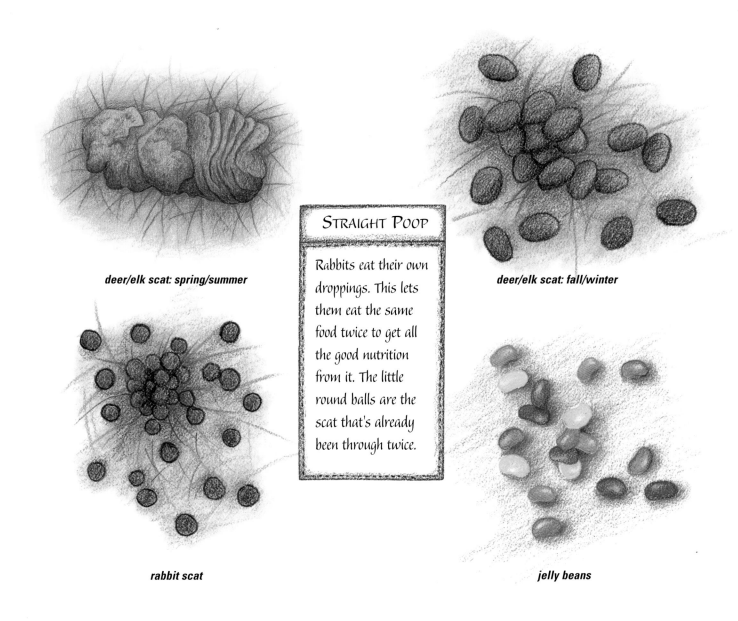

deer/elk scat: spring/summer

deer/elk scat: fall/winter

STRAIGHT POOP

Rabbits eat their own droppings. This lets them eat the same food twice to get all the good nutrition from it. The little round balls are the scat that's already been through twice.

rabbit scat

jelly beans

"That's not from a rabbit," said Mom, "It's from a deer."

"Right! Bunny poop looks like little round balls," added Dad. "Deer scat is shaped more like jellybeans."

"Are these deer tracks?" Michael asked.

"Yes!" said Mom. "See how they have split hooves?"

"Cool!" added Emily. She was starting to get interested.

"But what are these marks?"

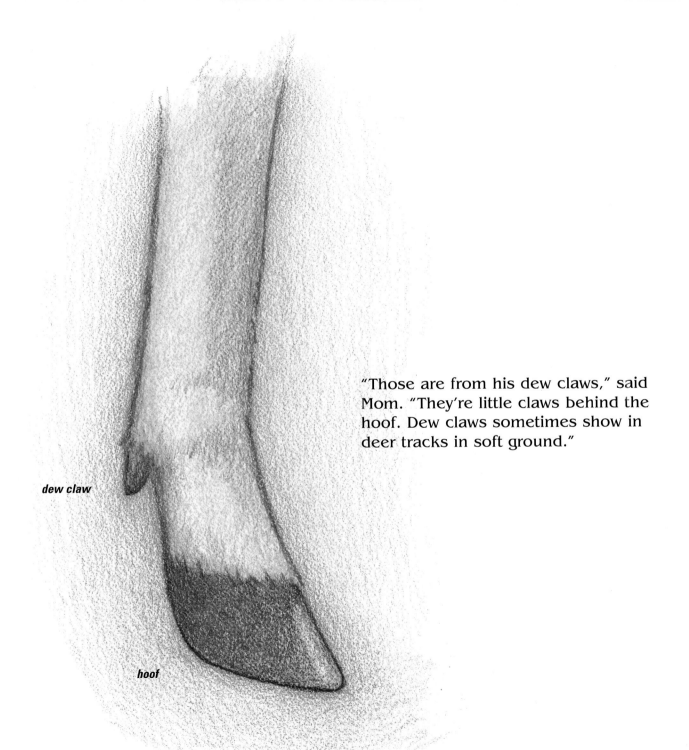

dew claw

hoof

"Those are from his dew claws," said Mom. "They're little claws behind the hoof. Dew claws sometimes show in deer tracks in soft ground."

STRAIGHT POOP

Female deer and elk don't grow antlers. Reindeer are the only members of the deer family where both males and females have antlers.

"Oh, no!" said Michael. "Here's one of his antlers. Did a bear eat him?" Michael looked around nervously.

"No, he's fine. Deer and elk shed their antlers every winter and then grow a new, bigger set the next year. This antler is from an elk."

"This elk was in a hurry, though," said Mom, as she studied the ground.

Michael and Emily went over to look.

"How can you tell?" said Michael.

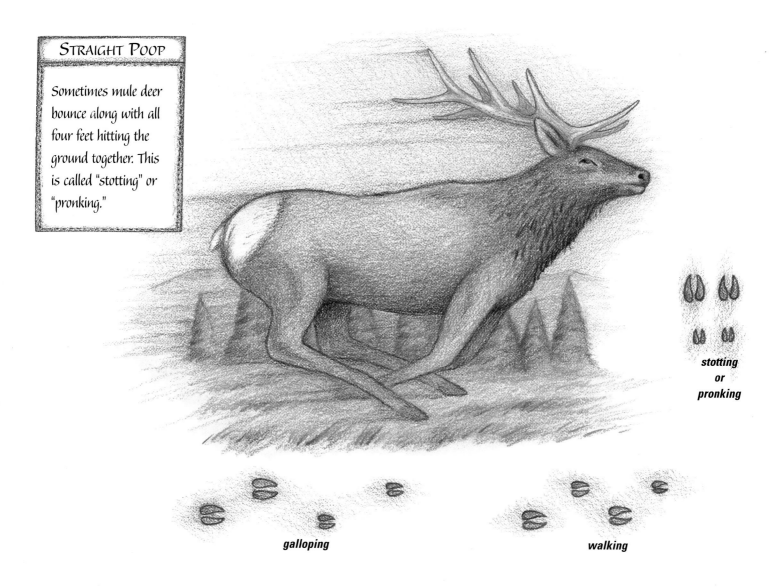

stotting
or
pronking

galloping

walking

"The hoofprints get very far apart here," Mom explained, "and the back prints are in front of the front prints."

"He was walking backwards?" said Emily.

"No, he was galloping. Something scared him and he was moving fast."

"I know what scared him," Dad called.

The family hurried over to look.

"This is coyote scat," Dad said, "and there are coyote tracks all around here."

"They look like dog tracks," said Michael.

"That's because coyotes are a member of the dog family," explained Dad.

"There were a lot of coyotes around here," said Mom.
"See how the tracks are different sizes?"

"Their den is probably nearby, and they scared the elk,"
Dad guessed.

"Did the coyotes get him?"
Michael asked.

"I don't think so," said Mom.
"Look!"

Far across the meadow, they
saw a family of coyotes, lying
in the sun.

As they walked along the trail into the woods,
Michael looked all over for tracks.

"Look, everyone! I found another coyote track."

coyote track

mountain lion track

"That's not a coyote track," said Dad. "It doesn't show any claw marks, and the front of the big pad looks dented in."

"You found a mountain lion track," said Mom.

"Let's look for mountain lion poop," said Michael.

"I don't think you'll find any," said Mom, "but you can look."

27

"Wow! There's a huge pile right here in the middle of the trail."

"That's not from a mountain lion. All you can see in it are vegetables and something that looks like oats," said Dad.

Horses walk while they poop, but they stop and stand still to pee.

"It's horse poop!" said Emily.

"Right," said Mom. "People ride horses out here. See if you can find any tracks."

Michael found tracks, all right, but they didn't look like he expected.

"That's an awfully funny-shaped hoof," he said.

"Horses don't have split hooves like elk and deer," said Dad,
"It's just one part."

"He means the shoe," said Mom.

Michael looked puzzled and Dad laughed. "Horses that are ridden a lot have metal shoes to keep their hooves from wearing down. That's the track you're seeing."

"What are these tracks over here?" asked Emily. She was kneeling by a hole in the ground looking at some tracks.

Dad took a close look. "Check out those long claw marks, kids!"

"Is it from a bear?" Michael said with a shudder.

"No," said Dad. "These are badger tracks, and that's
the hole he lives in."

"His claws are huge," said Emily.

"That's how he digs the holes," Mom answered. "He uses those front feet and claws like shovels and picks."

Michael followed the tracks backward from
the hole and spotted some big hoofprints.

"I found more deer prints over here!"

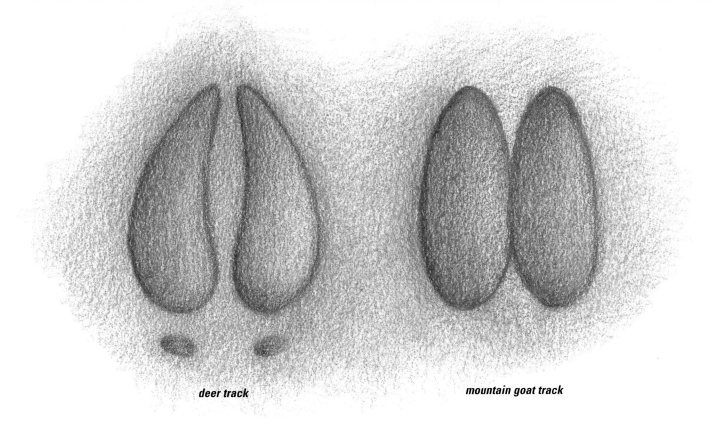

deer track

mountain goat track

"Those aren't deer prints," Dad pointed out. "They're not as pointy, and they don't turn in at the tips."

"Right," said Mom. "And they don't show dew claws. They're mountain goat tracks."

mountain goat scat

37

"Mountain goats usually spend the summer up in the high mountains," said Dad, "but they come down here, too."

"Whoa, Dad! What happened to this tree? Did an animal do that?"

"Something was sharpening its claws, Michael. And if you look how high those scratch marks go, it was pretty big!"

39

"It's not just the animal that's big," said Emily.
"Look at the size of this poop!"

"It looks like we found your grizzly bear," said Dad.
"Let's see what you learned today. What can you
figure out about this bear?"

"He's taller than you, and he has really long claws," said Michael.

"He's been eating plants," said Emily, "because there's no hair or bones in here."

"Good!" Mom said. "What else?"

STRAIGHT POOP

Grizzlies eat almost anything. They like fish and many kinds of plants, roots, and berries. Grizzlies can hunt their own meat, but they often steal kills away from wolves and other predators. They even eat moths and other insects.

"Here's his footprint," said Michael. "It's huge! He has more toes than a coyote, and his claws are longer than my fingers."

"I told you you'd be able to count a grizzly's toes," laughed Dad.

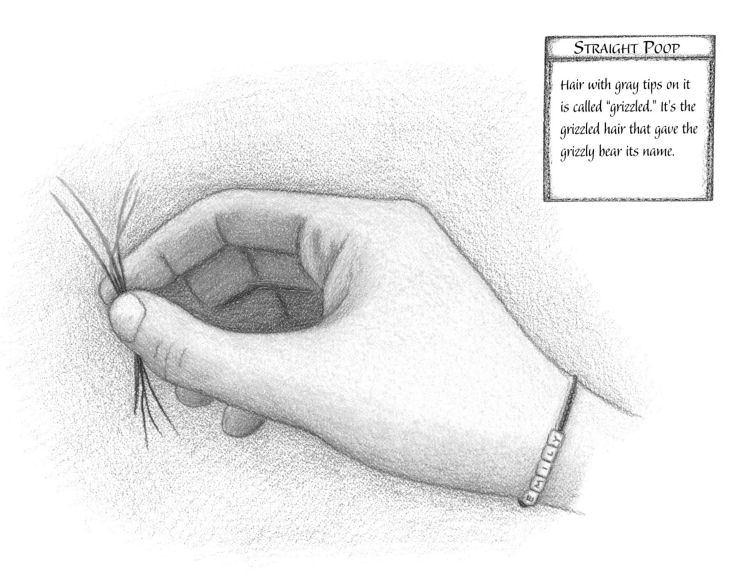

STRAIGHT POOP

Hair with gray tips on it is called "grizzled." It's the grizzled hair that gave the grizzly bear its name.

"He rubbed off some hair on the tree," said Emily. "It's really dark, but the tips are gray."

"Just like Dad's," smiled Mom.

"Don't pick on me," Dad grinned back.

As they ate dinner that night, everyone talked about how much fun they had.

"We didn't see very many animals," said Emily, "but it seemed like we did."

"And I didn't get scared once," said Michael.

Tracks and Scat Notes

Grizzly Bear
Very big tracks show large claw marks. Scat changes depending on diet. Claw marks show high on trees.

Rabbit
Small tracks filled in between toes. Scat is little balls.

Mule Deer
Pointy split-hoof tracks. Scat is made up of long ovals like jellybeans, not round like a rabbit's.

Elk
Tracks are longer and more blunt than that of a deer. Scat is quite a bit bigger than that of deer.

Horse
Tracks are almost as big as that of a bison or elk, but wider and not split. Scat is in chunks, with roughage from vegetation often visible.

Mountain Goat
Tracks are about the same size as deer tracks, but rounder and not turned in. Scat is pointier and bigger than that of a deer.

Beaver
Tracks are large, with slender toes and webbed hind feet, often obscured by dragging tail marks. Scat is rarely found.

Coyote
Tracks are like dog prints, with claws showing. Scat usually tapers off in long tails, and often contains hair and bones.

Mountain Lion
Tracks are almost as big as a wolf's, but claws don't show. Scat is rarely seen because they bury it.

Badger
Tracks show very long front claws connected to the toes. Scat is rarely seen.

The Author

Gary Robson lives in Montana near Yellowstone National Park, where he and his wife own a bookstore and tea bar. Gary has written dozens of books and hundreds of articles, mostly related to science, nature, and technology.
www.robson.org/gary

The Illustrator

Elijah Brady Clark has been passionate about design and illustration for as long as he can remember. After living his dream of traveling the United States in an Airstream Bambi Travel Trailer, he returned to northwestern Montana's Flathead Valley, where he grew up. He currently works as a designer and illustrator.

BOOKS IN THE WHO POOPED IN THE PARK? SERIES:

Acadia National Park
Big Bend National Park
Black Hills
Cascades
Colorado Plateau
Death Valley National Park
Glacier National Park
Grand Canyon National Park
Grand Teton National Park
Great Smoky Mountains National Park
Northwoods
Olympic National Park
Red Rock Canyon National Conservation Area
Rocky Mountain National Park
Sequoia and Kings Canyon National Parks
Shenandoah National Park
Sonoran Desert
Yellowstone National Park
Yosemite National Park